To my family,
and our love for Chile.

Story and illustrations by **Michelle Valenzuela Caorsi**

Roxy's
Big Chile Adventure

ROXY
BOOKS

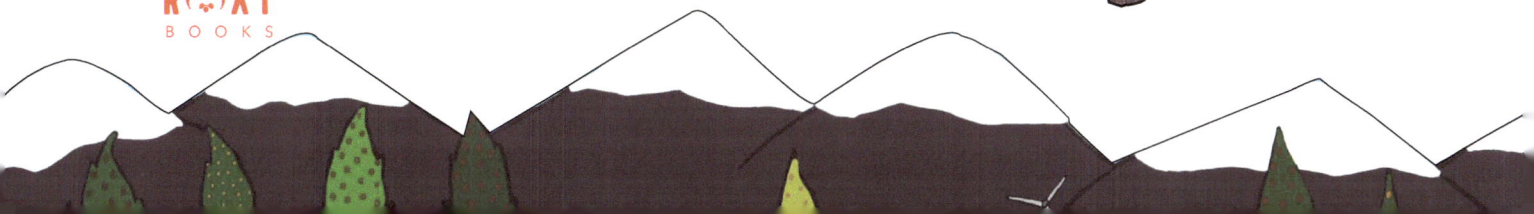

There is a long and narrow mysterious land in the southern corner of the world called Chile. Between its mighty Andes mountains covered with a white blanket of snow, and the Pacific Ocean's salty frothy waves that wash over the coasts, natural treasures can be found. From North to South, there are so many wonders to explore and animals to meet.

Roxy is one little furry friend that lives in Chile, and she is oh so curious. Don't be fooled by her cuteness and white fluffy coat that looks like a bundle of sugary cotton candy. She is a spunky dog that loves adventures. Today she is wearing a colorful flowered dress that is typically worn to celebrate important holidays.

What are you celebrating Roxy? "A new adventure", she says. "Follow me and you will see."

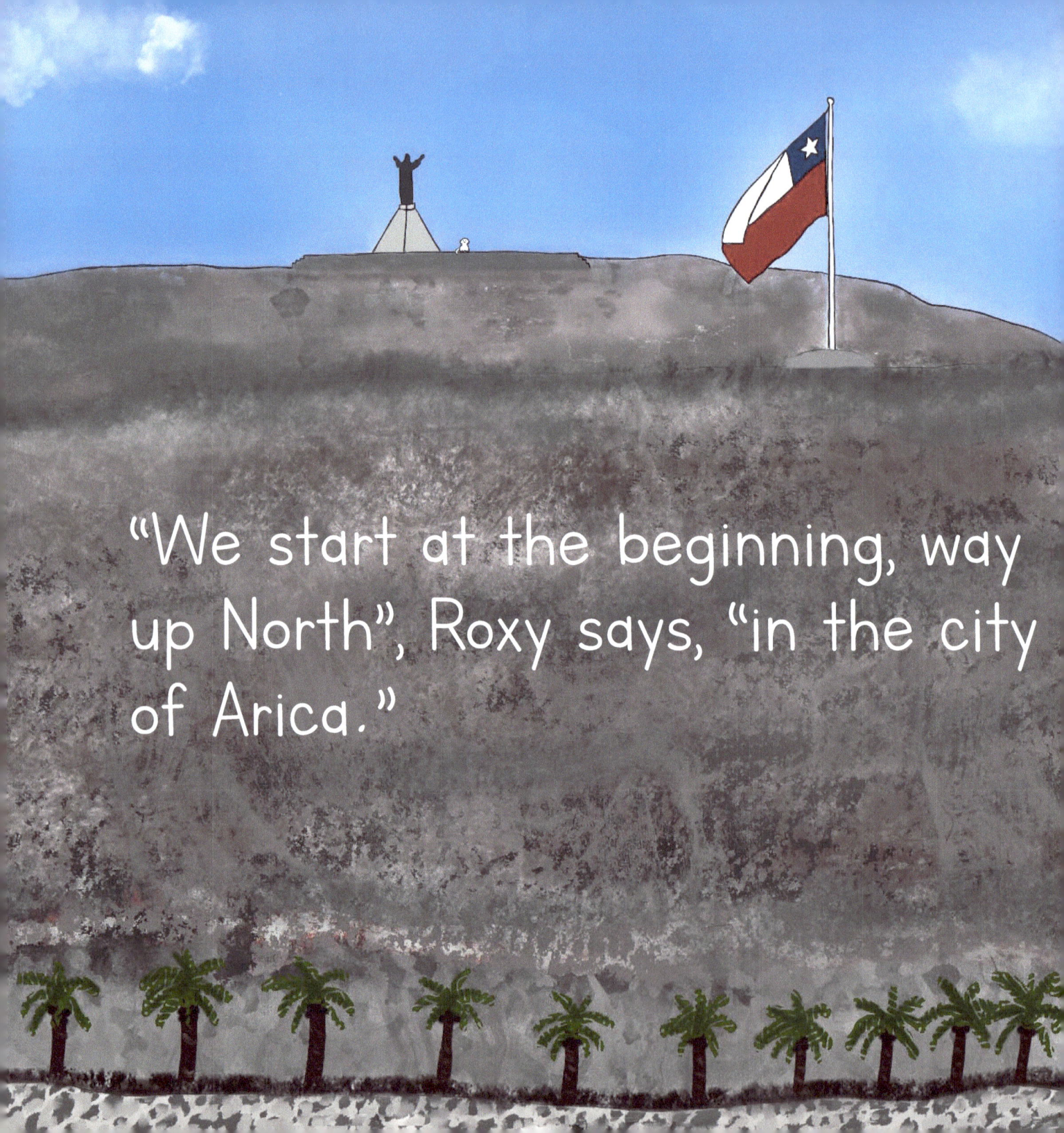

"We start at the beginning, way up North", Roxy says, "in the city of Arica."

This city with its palm trees and warm sunny beaches is a neighbor to a country called Peru.
The "morro de Arica" a very steep and high hill next to the ocean, is an important spot for tourists from all over of the world.
Like a rocky shield, it protects the city from the sea. Long ago there was a battle between Chile and Peru, and brave soldiers from both countries fought to defend their lands.
At the very top the Chilean flag flaps proud in the wind, with its solitary white star that represents the nation.

But where is Roxy, can you see her?

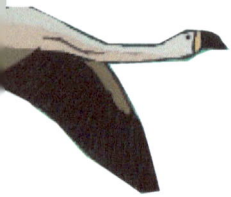

Next stop…… Chungará lake!
Roxy, did you know that
it is one of the highest lakes
in the world?

Its glassy waters are like a mirror that
reflect the white frosted volcanos and
scattered clouds that lazily float through
the pristine skies. It is a true oasis to
countless fauna, which means all the
animals that live in that area.
Roxy, there are so many new friends
to meet! What do you see?
"I see guanacos, an Andean fox, Chilean
flamingos and volcanos."

Marvelous!

Where are you now Roxy?

"Enjoying the crisp sea breeze with my new sea lion friend. This is Antofagasta, another northern city by the sea. I am admiring La Portada de Antofagasta which means a doorway to this land," Roxy says.

This natural arch was formed over millions of years with layers of fossils, shells, volcanic rocks, and other marine sediments. It looks so mysterious like a floating entry to a magical world.

What does it look like to you Roxy?

"Like a half-eaten chocolate frosted doughnut. I'm hungry".

Close to Antofagasta there are many copper deposits that are buried deep underground. In fact, Chile is the largest copper producer in the world! Copper is a very important mineral that is used to make things we use every day, like phones, computers, cars and much more. Copper helps electricity travel, and new technologies that take care of the environment such as solar and wind energy, need copper to build their parts. To collect the covered copper, big machines are needed to dig, shovel, and carry the rocks that have the red metal inside. Big pits are made, and giant trucks work busily non-stop like a long trail of ants that dig through the soil to build their mounds.

Where is Roxy? Who is her new friend?
It's a condor! Condors live in the Andes
range and can be found all over Chile. They are the
largest birds you will see flying in the sky.

High in the mountains,
hot springs bubble and boil
under the ground.

The water gets so hot, it squirts out of holes in the ground like a giant fountain with dancing spouts that plumet to the soil as its grand finale. The steam forms a white smoky curtain that seems like the clouds have reached the earth. These are the Tatio Geysers, a splendid sight to see in the early hours of the day. Roxy, what do you think of this natural phenomenon? "There is vapor all around, but the temperature is very cold. I wore my coat to keep me warm."

This is a sight I won't forget. It's like an enormous cake that had its candles blown out. I suddenly crave a piece of cake," says Roxy.

When the conditions are right, something magical happens in the desert.
It blooms! But how can that be?

Hundreds of different kinds of wildflowers make their appearance only if there has been enough rainfall to awaken the seeds that have been quietly sleeping under the dry desert soil. When they begin to sprout, the desert bursts with a festival of colors, like an overstuffed piñata that ruptures spilling multicolored sweets on the ground. The rainbow of blossoms attracts lizards, insects, and animals, turning the once quiet empty desert, into a busy landscape of enchantment.

What a treat for Roxy!

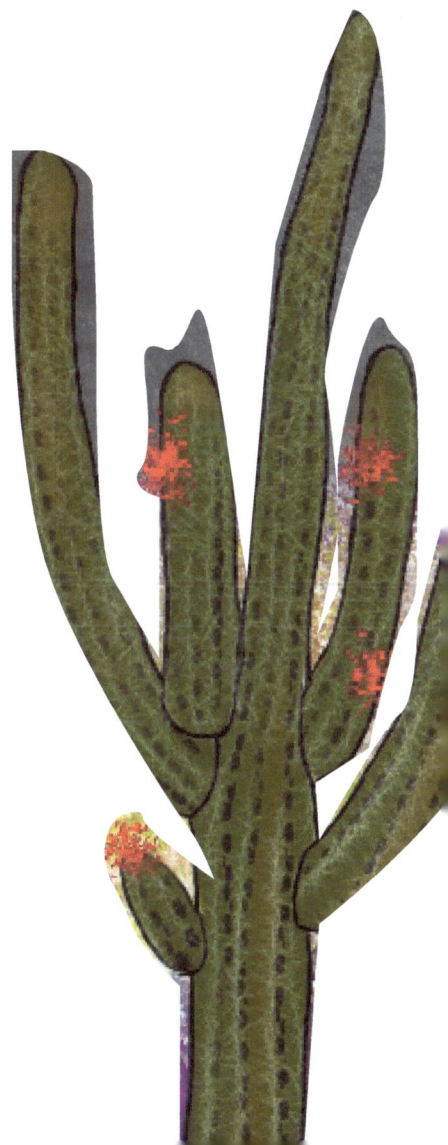

Roxy continues her journey heading south but stops in the path to the stars in Valle del Elqui. Here the skies are so transparent, astronomers travel from faraway places to study the cosmos. When the sun sets at the end of each day, millions of stars begin to flicker, lighting the night like summer fireflies that awake at dusk and spatter the darkness with their playful glow. Roxy made a new friend, a tiny chinchilla that keeps her company while she observes the dreamy nebula up above.

Roxy has made it to the big metropolis of Santiago!

There is so much hustle and bustle, noises, and crowds. So many buildings in the capital city, and home to the tallest skyscraper in South America. It reaches for the clouds, and towers over the other buildings in the city's skyline. Roxy visits Cerro San Cristobal, a metropolitan park that sits on a lush hill and has cable cars that carry visitors over treetops to enjoy a clear view. But where is Roxy, can you find her?

Not too far from Santiago on the Pacific's coast, there's a unique historic city built in the hillsides called Valparaiso. It has colorful houses, long winding streets, endless staircases, bright urban art, funicular railways, and countless cafés and ice cream shops. There is so much to do, and so much to see. Roxy wants to get a better view, so she takes flight paragliding through the skies swaying from side to side. What an adventure Roxy!

Far from the mainland in the middle of the ocean Rapa Nui, a Chilean volcanic island, emerges from the blue waters. Also called Easter Island, it can only be reached by plane or by boat. Roxy soars and zips through the sky, like a condor with its outstretched wings. Oh, what a sight down below, the mighty moai stand so tall and so proud. For hundreds of years, they have been watching over and protecting the islanders. But how did they get there? Roxy imagines they marched out of the depths of a fiery volcano and stood with their backs to the sea, forming a protective barrier against the pacific winds that whistle and blow with all their might.

Back on the mainland Roxy
hops on a train headed south.

Outside the window the rolling hills with an abundance of juicy fruit whiz by, blending into a kaleidoscope of colors. Roxy is getting closer to Santa Cruz, where vineyards are bountiful, and grapes ripen to perfection. When the time is right, the grapes are smooshed for their juices, and placed to rest in golden oak barrels for many days and nights. The wood's spicy aroma gives the wine that's fermenting within, a delicate flavor. Roxy visits a vineyard and decides to take a closer look at how the vines grow.

Can you spot Roxy?

Roxy keeps heading south to the Araucanía Region, a territory in Chile that is rich with lakes, rivers, volcanos, and beautiful araucaria trees. The araucarias are sacred evergreen trees with a long trunk, and branches that reach out to the sky forming a ruffled green umbrella to shelter all the living creatures below. Roxy meets two new friends in the araucaria forest; a tiny pudú, the smallest deer there is, and a large strong huemul, that is also part of the deer family. They are both so shy, and they hide behind the branches until they feel it's safe to come out. But Roxy is tiny too, and soon they become friends. The pudú and huemul tell her what it's like to live in the forest.

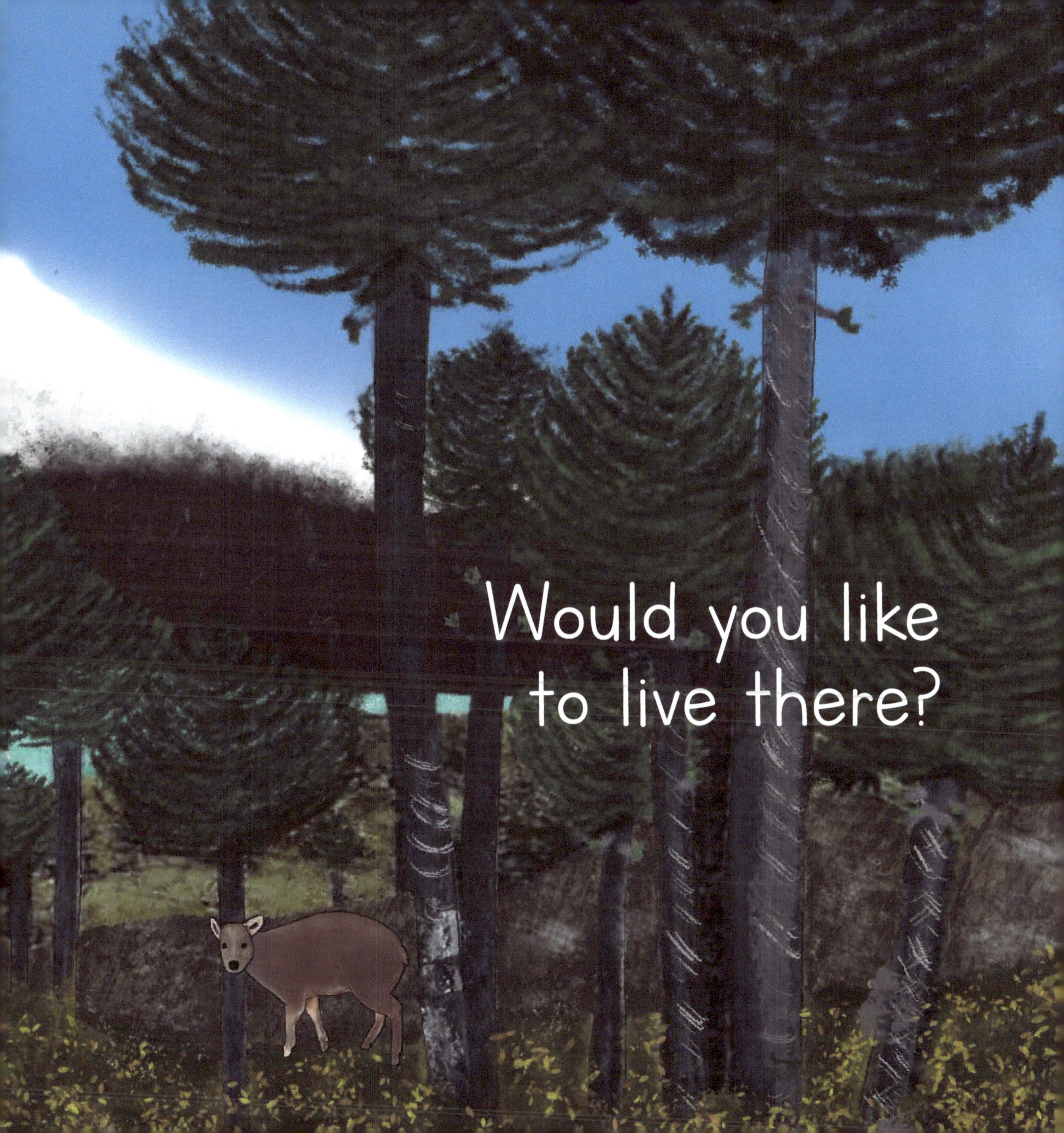

Would you like
to live there?

The Chiloe archipelago is a must-see destination.

Every spring and summer the cool Humboldt currents carry the large humpback whale over long distances in search of food. Its distinguishable underwater song is a melancholic and serene symphony for all the aquatic animals of the area. Toninas, Chilean Dolphins, enjoy their concert as they surf through the blue-green waves. Roxy speeds by on an artisanal boat to get a closer look of the chatty Humboldt penguins, that nest on an islet alongside many other bird and penguin species. Such a diversity of fauna that has Chile as its home!

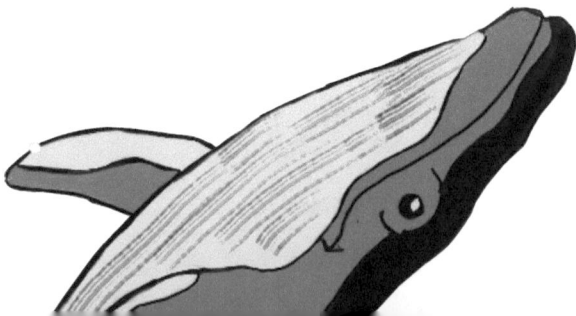

Roxy's continues her travels to San Rafael Lake, a very original lake that leaves Roxy speechless!

She boards a white and red boat to take her closer to the blue-frozen wall that floats over the icy waters. The glacier of San Rafael Lake has been forming over hundreds of years, with its crystalline peaks and white frosted edges.

It lazily glides over the water, and when a chunk suddenly breaks off, it splashes with an enormous thunder. The noise and the waves frighten Roxy, and she feels so small next to the towering blocks of ice.

What do you think Roxy?

"I'm ready to warm up with a nice cup of hot cocoa," she says.

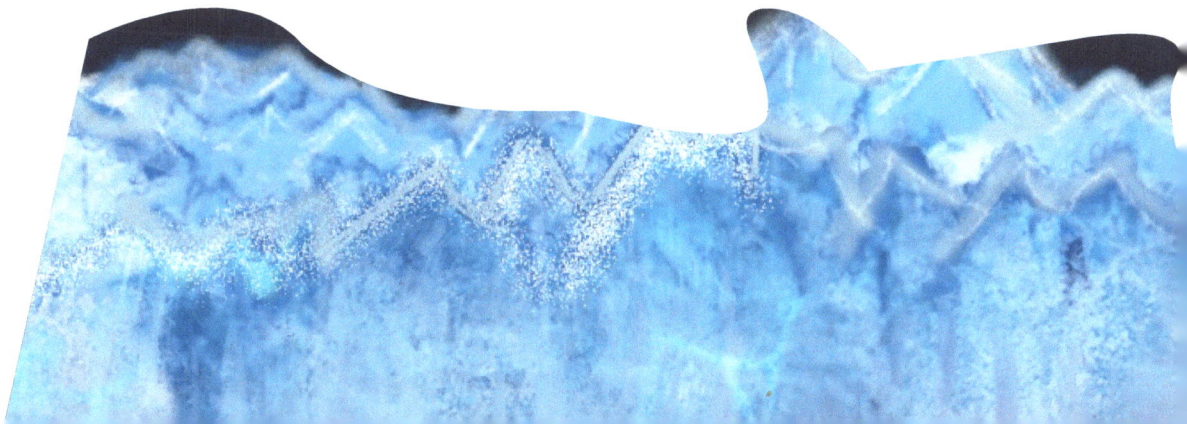

"Come fly with me, and a most spectacular thing you will see," says the mighty condor gliding over the pointy granite peaks of Torres del Paine.

Torres means towers, and Roxy admires
their size and shape while spotting
a lonely puma in the distance.
It is windy and cold, yet this austral
region is home to so many animals.
Roxy starts thinking of her own home
in the big capital city, and her cozy bed
that is waiting for her to snuggle and
dream of new adventures.
That is where she belongs, and it's time
to head back. Chile has been quite a
discovery, and Roxy will never forget
about her journey through
each different region
or the new friends she met.

The End

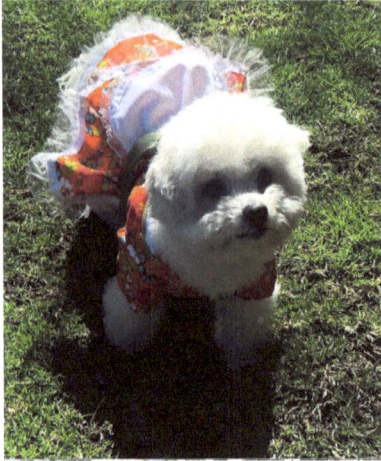

Roxy's
Big Chile Adventure

STORY AND ILLUSTRATIONS BY
Michelle Valenzuela Caorsi
roxybookseditorial@gmail.com

GRAPHIC DESIGN
SOLOUNO DISEÑO GRAFICO
www.solouno.cl
@solouno_disenografico
kathysp@solouno.cl

ISBN

978-1-7378363-3-9

ROXY
B O O K S

ABOUT THE AUTHOR

Michelle was born in Washington, D.C.,
and in her early years she lived in
Switzerland, El Salvador, Peru, and later
returned to the Washington Metropolitan
area where she continued her studies.
She has a Bachelor's Degree in English, a
Master's of Education, and is
a certified simultaneous interpreter.
She has a background in teaching,
and is currently working as an interpreter
and translator in diverse industries.

www.ingramcontent.com/pod-product-compliance
Lightning Source LLC
LaVergne TN
LVHW072055070426
835508LV00002B/114